A Science/Literature Unit
Guide for Using

# The Magic School Bus® Inside the Earth

in the Cla

*Based on the book writ*

*This guide written by*

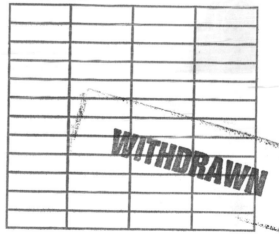

**DATE DUE**

WITHDRAWN

*Teacher Created Materials,*
6421 Industry Way
Westminster, CA 92683
www.teachercreated.com

©*1996 Teacher Created Ma*
Reprinted, 2001

Made in U.S.A.
**ISBN-1-55734-544-9**

Teacher
Created
Materials

# Table of Contents

**Introduction** . . . . . . . . . . . . . . . . . . . . . . . . . . . . . . . . . . . . . . . . . . . . . 3

**Before the Book** (Pre-reading Activities) . . . . . . . . . . . . . . . . . . . . . . . . 4

**About the Author** . . . . . . . . . . . . . . . . . . . . . . . . . . . . . . . . . . . . . . . . . 5

**Book Summary** . . . . . . . . . . . . . . . . . . . . . . . . . . . . . . . . . . . . . . . . . . . 6

**Hands-On Lessons**

   ✦ Rocks and Minerals . . . . . . . . . . . . . . . . . . . . . . . . . . . . . . . . . . . 7

      *(Distinguishing Between Rocks and Minerals)*

   ✦ The Earth's Crust . . . . . . . . . . . . . . . . . . . . . . . . . . . . . . . . . . . . 9

      *(Observing Soil and Sand)*

   ✦ Sedimentary Rock . . . . . . . . . . . . . . . . . . . . . . . . . . . . . . . . . . . 11

      *(Making Simulated Sedimentary Rock)*

   ✦ Caves . . . . . . . . . . . . . . . . . . . . . . . . . . . . . . . . . . . . . . . . . . . . . 13

      *(Creating a Diorama of a Cave)*

   ✦ Metamorphic Rock . . . . . . . . . . . . . . . . . . . . . . . . . . . . . . . . . . 18

      *(Making Simulated Metamorphic Rock)*

   ✦ Igneous Rock . . . . . . . . . . . . . . . . . . . . . . . . . . . . . . . . . . . . . . . 19

      *(Making Simulated Igneous Rock)*

   ✦ Layers of the Earth . . . . . . . . . . . . . . . . . . . . . . . . . . . . . . . . . . 20

      *(Making a Cutaway Model of the Earth)*

   ✦ The Moving Crust . . . . . . . . . . . . . . . . . . . . . . . . . . . . . . . . . . . 26

      *(Investigating Crustal Movement)*

   ✦ Volcanoes . . . . . . . . . . . . . . . . . . . . . . . . . . . . . . . . . . . . . . . . . 33

      *(Simulating Volcanic Eruption)*

   ✦ Rock Cycle . . . . . . . . . . . . . . . . . . . . . . . . . . . . . . . . . . . . . . . . 36

      *(Walking Through the Rock Cycle)*

**After the Book** (Post-reading Activity)

   ✦ Identifying Minerals . . . . . . . . . . . . . . . . . . . . . . . . . . . . . . . . . . 38

**Unit Assessment** . . . . . . . . . . . . . . . . . . . . . . . . . . . . . . . . . . . . . . . . . 40

**Resources**

   ✦ Related Books and Periodicals . . . . . . . . . . . . . . . . . . . . . . . . . . 44

   ✦ Related Materials . . . . . . . . . . . . . . . . . . . . . . . . . . . . . . . . . . . . 45

**Answer Key** . . . . . . . . . . . . . . . . . . . . . . . . . . . . . . . . . . . . . . . . . . . . . 46

**Glossary** . . . . . . . . . . . . . . . . . . . . . . . . . . . . . . . . . . . . . . . . . . . . . . . 48

# Introduction

The use of literature can enhance the study of science. The key to selecting these books is to check them for scientific accuracy and appropriateness for the level of the students. *The Magic School Bus®* series, written by Joanna Cole, is an outstanding example of books which can help students enjoy and learn about science. These books are delightfully written and scientifically accurate, thanks to the thorough research done by the author.

This *Science/Literature Unit* is directly related to *The Magic School Bus® Inside the Earth.* It is designed to help you present exciting lessons for your students so that they can develop their understanding and appreciation of the earth and its structure. The activities in this unit are particularly appropriate for intermediate and middle grades.

## Internet Extenders

Today, many classrooms are connected to the Internet, a technology which puts students in touch with worldwide resources. As with selecting the literature for this unit, the author of the unit has searched the Internet to find quality Web sites that directly relate to the topics covered in this book. This supplemental information helps to expand the students' knowledge of the topic, as well as make them aware of the many valuable resources to be found on the Internet. Some Web sites lend themselves to group research; others are best viewed by the entire class. If available, use a large screen monitor when the entire class is viewing a Web site and discussing its content. *Internet Extenders* are included throughout the unit. These are special sections which note outstanding Web sites and include suggestions for incorporating Web site information into the lessons. Where appropriate, a *Technology Extender,* such as the use of video cameras, may be suggested in the lessons.

Although these Web sites have been carefully selected, they may not exist forever. One method of assuring that Web site information will continue to be available for a class is to use a program (if available) or browser which enables one to download and save a single Web page or entire site. Teacher Created Materials attempts to offset the ongoing problem of sites which move, "go dark," or otherwise leave the Internet after a book has been printed. If you attempt to contact a Web site listed in this unit and find that it no longer exists, check the TCM home page at *www.teachercreated.com* for updated URL's for this book.

# The Earth

Before you begin reading *The Magic School Bus® Inside the Earth*, complete the activities "What Is Inside the Earth?" and "How Are Rocks Formed?"

## What Is Inside the Earth?

Ms. Frizzle is about to take her class on another wild adventure study trip, this time to explore the inside of the planet Earth. The Friz put her students to work writing reports on the earth and then assigned them to bring a rock to class the next day.

The Friz asked her class, "Don't you often wonder what is inside the earth?" What do you think is inside the earth? Use this circle to draw a view of the inside of the earth without looking up the answer in any books. Save this picture to look at again at the end of this study after you have learned more about the earth.

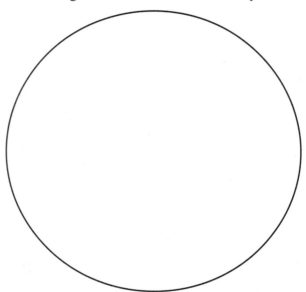

Cutaway View of the Earth

## How Are Rocks Formed?

On the lines below, write a brief description of how you think rocks are made. On the back of this PaPer, include drawings to help explain your ideas.

_____

_____

_____

_____

_____

_____

_____

# About the Author

Joanna Cole was born on August 11, 1944, in New York. She attended the University of Massachusetts and Indiana University before receiving her B.A. from the City College of University of New York in 1967.

Joanna Cole loved science as a child. "I always enjoyed explaining things and writing reports for school. I had a teacher who was a little like Ms. Frizzle. She loved her subject. Every week she had a child do an experiment in front of the room and I wanted to be that child every week," she recalls. It's no surprise that Cole's favorite book as a child was *Bugs, Insects, and Such.*

Ms. Cole has worked as an elementary school teacher, a librarian, and a children's book editor. Combining her knowledge of children's literature with her love of science, she decided to write children's books. Her first book was *Cockroaches* (1971), which she wrote because there had never been a children's book written about the insect before. "I had ample time to study the creature in my low-budget New York apartment!"

Teachers and students have praised Joanna Cole's ability to make science interesting and understandable. Her *Magic School Bus®* series has now made science funny, as well. Cole says that before she wrote this series, she had a goal to write good science books, telling stories that would be so much fun to read that readers would read them even without the science components.

Readers across the country love *The Magic School Bus®* series and enjoy following the adventures of the wacky science teacher, Ms. Frizzle. Joanna Cole works closely with Bruce Degen, the illustrator for this series, to create fascinating and scientifically accurate books for children.

Even a successful writer sometimes finds it scary to begin writing a new book. That was the way Cole felt before beginning to write *The Magic School Bus®* series. She says, "I couldn't work at all. I cleaned out closets, answered letters, went shopping—anything but sit down and write. But eventually I did it, even though I was scared."

Joanna Cole says young people often write their own *Magic School Bus®* adventures. She suggests they just pick a topic and a place for a field trip. Do a lot of research about the topic. Think of a story line and make it funny. Some students even like to put their own teachers into their stories.

# The Magic School Bus®
# Inside the Earth

### by Joanna Cole

*(Canada, Scholastic; U.K, Scholastic Limited; AUS, Ashton Scholastic Party Limited)*

When Ms. Frizzle announces to her class that they will be studying the earth and then asks them to write reports and bring in rock specimens, the students are not very excited. In fact, only four students bring their rocks to school the next day, and only one specimen was really a rock. But never fear; The Friz knows just how to get her students excited about studying rocks and the earth—by taking them on another wild field trip aboard Ms. Frizzle's magic bus.

After they climb aboard the bus, it suddenly begins spinning. When it stops, the students and Ms. Frizzle are dressed in miners' outfits, and the bus turns into a steam shovel. "Start digging!" commands The Friz, and soon they are shoveling away the layers of soil. Before long, they hit hard rock and have to use jackhammers to break through it. They identify the rock layers beneath the soil as sedimentary rocks.

The class begins to find many fossils in these layers, but Ms. Frizzle tells them to get back on the bus. They board just in time as the ground begins to collapse beneath the bus, and it falls into a cave. There, they discover minerals in the shapes of icicles hanging from the ceiling and growing up from the floor. There is not enough time to explore this cave, however, since the bus has now sprouted a huge drill and begins to bore through the rock.

As the bus and class go deeper the air becomes hotter. The rocks have changed too; because of the heat and pressure, they have become much harder and have become metamorphic rocks.

The bus continues to go even deeper toward the center of the earth. The students and Ms. Frizzle discover granite, an igneous rock which was formed billions of years ago. More rock samples are added to their collection. They board the bus which drills deeper and deeper. It becomes much hotter as they zoom toward the center of the earth. Once they reach the center, Ms. Frizzle steers the bus out of it and drives straight up through a tunnel of black rock.

The students are surprised to find themselves driving out of a volcano which is an island. They get out and examine the volcanic rocks. Suddenly, the volcano rumbles to life, and molten lava begins to flow from it, carrying the bus, teacher, and students toward the sea. A parachute sprouts from the bus, and it rises high on the cloud of steam created when the lava cools as it pours into the sea. From there, the bus floats back to the school parking lot.

Back at school, the students make a display of their rock specimens. They identify them and tell some of the ways they are used. How exciting their study of rocks and the earth has been, thanks to the magic bus.

# Rocks and Minerals

Ms. Frizzle started her study of the earth by having each student bring in a rock. Some of the class brought things which were not rocks. It is not only difficult to know what a rock is, but it is even more challenging to know what the difference is between a rock and a mineral. A rock is made of minerals, but minerals are made of chemical elements or compounds. Use a cookie to help yourself understand the difference.

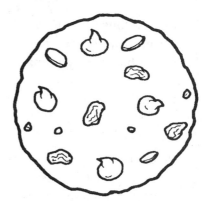

**To the Teacher:** You will need to purchase or make cookies for the students, which contain a variety of ingredients (e.g., raisins, chocolate chips, nuts, coconut).

**To the Students:** Pretend the cookie is a rock and pull it apart to find the "minerals" inside it. Use just half of the cookie and save the rest for later. Carefully break the half cookie into pieces. Separate the materials which you find in your cookie, such as nuts or raisins, into the different rectangles below.

|  |  |  |
|---|---|---|
| _____ | _____ | _____ |
| _____ | _____ | _____ |

The different materials in the cookie rock represent minerals. Write the names of the minerals you found in the cookie on the blank lines at the bottom of the rectangles.

**Closure:** Now you can do something with your cookie rock that you cannot do with a real one. You can eat it!

**Extender:** Tim's report "What Are Rocks Made Of?" stated that "Rocks are made of minerals." Scientists classify minerals by their color, texture, luster, density, hardness, and streak. Sometimes they even use their sense of smell or taste to describe some minerals. This helps them tell one mineral from another. You can do this too in the activity on page 8 ("Can You Find My Mineral?").

# Can You Find My Mineral?

**To the Teacher:** You may wish to supply mineral samples for the students, in addition to the specimens they bring from home. See the Related Material section (page 45) for a source of minerals. Note: To determine hardness you may wish to have students use the Mohs Hardness Scale in which minerals are scratched by a fingernail, a penny, a streak plate (glass) or knife blade, and a steel nail. Hardness is determined as follows: fingernail = 2.5 or less, penny = 3 or less, glass or knife = 5.5 or less, steel nail = 6.5 or less. If none of the above materials scratch the mineral, the hardness is determined to be greater than 6.5.

**To the Students:** Now it is your turn to bring a rock to school. Try to find one which is made up of all one mineral. Write a clear description of your mineral on the file card so that someone else can easily find it after it is mixed with the other specimens.

**Materials:** mineral samples, penny, steel nail, unglazed tile, lined 3" x 5" file card

**Procedure:** Write each characteristic title on a different line of the file card. Choose the words which best describe your mineral for each characteristic and write them beside the title. When you are finished, add your mineral to the others and mix them up. Exchange your card with another student and see whether he or she can find your mineral and you can find the other.

| Characteristic | | Description |
|---|---|---|
| **Color** | — | What color or colors can you see in your mineral? |
| **Texture** | — | Feel your mineral. Is it rough, smooth, soapy, or bumpy? |
| **Luster** | — | Look at the surface of the mineral. Is it shiny, glassy, metallic, dull, or chalky? |
| **Density** | — | Is your rock heavier or lighter than you would expect for its size? If it is the weight that you would expect for its size, just write "average weight." |
| **Hardness** | — | Use your fingernail, a penny, unglazed tile, and steel nail to see if you can make a scratch on the mineral. Scratch the mineral with your fingernail first. If it does not leave a scratch, try the penny. Continue with the others in the order listed until one of them leaves a scratch. Write the name of what scratched the material. If nothing scratched it, the mineral was harder than all of these; write "hard." |
| **Streak** | — | Hold the unglazed tile and rub the rock across it. If a streak of color rubs off, write down the color. Write "no streak color" if the rock does not leave a streak. |

---

### Internet Extender

**Activity Summary:** Find information on how to identify minerals, create a collection, grow salt crystals, and check how much you know about minerals.

**San Diego Natural History Mineral Matters—Kid's Habitat:**

*http://www.sdnhm.org/kids/minerals/cover.html*

- Click on *How to Identify Minerals* to get details for describing the characteristics of minerals.
- Click on *Create a Collection* to get helpful hints for cleaning, sorting, and displaying your mineral specimens.
- Click on *Grow Your Own Minerals* to see how to grow salt crystals.
- Click on *Mine Games* and choose from the list of activities to test your mineral knowledge.

---

# Looking at Dirt

When the bus stopped spinning, it had become a steam shovel. The students and Ms. Frizzle were now dressed as miners with picks and shovels. The Friz told the students to start digging through the top layer of the earth's crust, which is what we call dirt or soil. Florrie wrote the report "What Is Soil?" to list the ingredients which make up soil. Let's do a scientific investigation of soil.

**Materials:** three soil samples, magnifying glass, clear tape

**Procedure:** Collect samples of soil from the school and home areas, as well as commercial potting soil. Place about two teaspoons (10 mL) of each sample in a different plastic bag and mark on the bag where you collected the specimen.

Use clear tape to stick a sample specimen from each of the soils you have collected on the chart. Make notes of your examination of the soil samples and list the minerals you found in them. Also, make drawings of the view you had through the magnifying glass or a microscope.

|  | A | B | C |
|---|---|---|---|
| **Soil Sample** |  |  |  |
| **Location of Sample** |  |  |  |
| **Things I Found in the Soil Sample** |  |  |  |
| **Drawing of Magnified Soil Sample** |  |  |  |

# Looking at Sand

Now that you know what soil looks like, collect three different samples of sand and compare it to soil.

**Materials:** three sand samples, magnifying glass, clear tape

**Procedure:** Collect three sand samples and examine them, using a magnifying glass to show the details needed to complete the chart below. Tape a sample of each sand specimen to the chart and then examine each one carefully and report what you find on the chart.

|  | A | B | C |
|---|---|---|---|
| **Sand Sample** |  |  |  |
| **Location of Sample** |  |  |  |
| **Drawing of Magnified Soil Sample** (Including colors) |  |  |  |

**Closure:** Write two ways in which sand and soil are similar and two ways in which they are different.

| **Similar** | **Different** |
|---|---|
| _____ | _____ |
| _____ | _____ |

How do you think soil is formed? _____

_____

How do you think sand is formed?_____

_____

# Simulated Sedimentary Rock

Ms. Frizzle's students discovered layers in the rock as they dug deeper into the earth's crust. They labeled the minerals in these layers as sandstone, shale, and limestone. The Friz explained that these are sedimentary rock layers. The report which Molly wrote, "How Rock Layers Were Formed," stated that these were laid down millions of years ago. You examined sand in the "Looking at Sand" activity and discovered that it was really tiny particles of rocks. The rocks were broken down by wind, water, and extreme temperatures; this is called *weathering*. As the rock particles piled up in layers, they eventually pressed together until they became solid rock.

As The Friz explained, sand pressed together in this way creates *sandstone*. Mud and clay pressed together make *shale*. Another type of sedimentary rock is made from shells of mollusks, such as clams and oysters, which partially consist of calcium carbonate, a kind of lime. As these animals died, their shells drifted to the ocean floor and were packed down in layers which became *limestone*.

Simulate layers of sedimentary rock by following the directions below.

**Materials:** two or three pieces of chalk, dirt, sand, large clear glass jar

**Procedure:** Fill the jar about ¼ full with water to represent the ocean. Grind the chalk into small pieces and drop them into the jar. Gradually add layers of the material to the "ocean," as follows. Each layer should be about ½ inch (1.3 cm) deep. Be sure to let each layer settle before adding the next one.

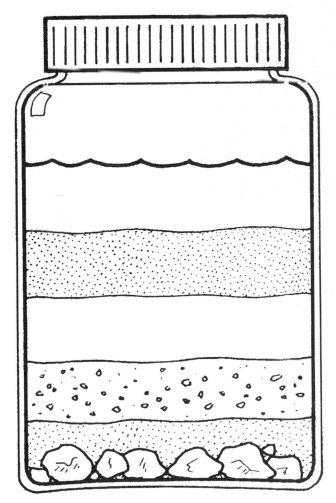

1. The ocean waves break large rocks into small particles, which become sand. Pour sand into the ocean.

2. A river carries silt from its banks into the ocean. Add the dirt to simulate this.

3. Shells of dead mollusks fall to the bottom of the ocean. Add the chalk to represent the shells of tiny animals.

4. More sand is laid down and then more dirt is washed on top of it. Add another layer of sand and then dirt.

**Closure:** In nature, these layers become more and more compressed as other materials are added and eventually change to rock after thousands of years. The rock layers may be lifted up above the water level and exposed. You can sometimes see these rock layers where roads, streams, or rivers have cut through them.

# Sedimentary Sandwich

Make a sandwich to show how the layers of the sedimentary rock might look and to demonstrate how fossils may be embedded in rock.

**Materials:** one slice each of dark and whole wheat bread, smooth peanut butter, cream cheese, three or four small celery leaves, chocolate bar with nuts, spreading knife

**Procedure:** Add the layers of simulated rock as follows.

1. *Begin with the piece of whole wheat bread as the granite level,* igneous rock laid down billions of years ago.

2. Shells of dead mollusks sink to the ocean floor. *Spread the cream cheese to represent the limestone which results from the crushed shells being pressed and cemented together as they mix with sea water.*

3. Over millions of years, this part of the floor of the ocean is gradually raised, becoming dry land. Eventually, the limestone is flooded by water, creating a shallow lake. Mud washes into the lake and covers some live animals. The soft body parts decay away and their bones are gradually replaced by minerals which then harden into stone. The bone is then fossilized. The mud hardens into shale. *Place the chocolate bar with nuts over the limestone to represent the shale and fossils.*

4. Leaves wash into the lake and are trapped between the shale and sandstone. *Spread a thick layer of peanut butter on the dark bread to represent sandstone. Make the peanut butter as smooth as possible and then place several celery leaves on top of the peanut butter and gently press them down. Carefully remove the leaves and then lay this layer, peanut butter side down, over the layer of shale.* Fossil imprints of leaves were sometimes made when they fell to the ground and were gradually covered by additional layers of sand or dirt. The leaf decayed and disappeared, leaving only its print in the sand layer above it, which eventually became sandstone. *The dark bread represents topsoil which is deposited on the layers after the lake disappear.s and the layers are raised again.*

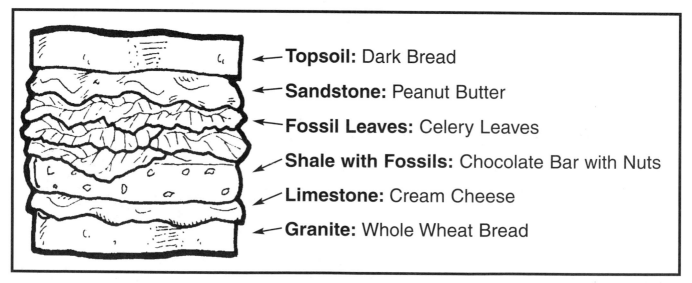

**Topsoil:** Dark Bread

**Sandstone:** Peanut Butter

**Fossil Leaves:** Celery Leaves

**Shale with Fossils:** Chocolate Bar with Nuts

**Limestone:** Cream Cheese

**Granite:** Whole Wheat Bread

**Closure:** Carefully separate the sandwich layers between the shale and sandstone layers to look for the fossil leaf imprints and then break open the shale to discover the fossils (nuts) hidden inside. Now, you can eat the layers of sedimentary rock.

# Caves

Just as the students were finding many fossils, Ms. Frizzle told them to get back on the bus. Suddenly, as they were driving, they heard rock crumbling underneath them. They were falling through a dark hole into the earth! Bump! They had landed in a huge limestone cave.

## Cave Facts

Most caves are made of limestone layers which have been dissolved by rain water. As shown in the pictures below, rain water drips down through cracks in the rocks and combines with underground water.

Rain picks up carbon dioxide as it falls, and then it mixes with leaves and other materials in the soil, changing the water to a weak carbonic acid.

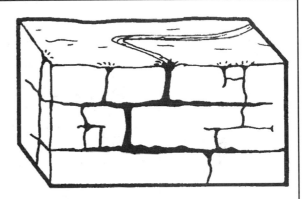

Over thousands of years, the acid gradually dissolves the limestone rocks, leaving crevices.

The crevices are made larger by water rushing through the cave and by rock slides. This can leave huge underground rooms and tunnels.

**To the Teacher:** The activities which follow will help students understand how caves are created, as well as what they look like. Use the pictures on this page to show the students the process which creates caves naturally and then conduct the lessons so they can simulate this process.

# How Is a Cave Created?

Do an experiment to see how limestone can be dissolved by a weak acid. You will use an egg since the shell of an egg is mostly calcium carbonate, the same material which makes limestone. Carbonic acid, created when rain water mixes with carbon dioxide and decaying organic material in the soil, is like the acetic acid in vinegar.

**Materials:** white vinegar, dropper, uncooked egg in its shell, clear plastic cup

**Procedure:** Place the egg in the plastic cup and add enough vinegar to cover it. Observe and make drawings on the chart below to show what is happening to the egg.

| | |
|---|---|
| **Date/Time:** _____<br><br>**Comments:** <br><br>_____<br><br>_____<br><br>_____<br><br>_____ | **Date/Time:** _____<br><br>**Comments:** <br><br>_____<br><br>_____<br><br>_____<br><br>_____ |
| **Date/Time:** _____<br><br>**Comments:** <br><br>_____<br><br>_____<br><br>_____<br><br>_____ | **Date/Time:** _____<br><br>**Comments:** <br><br>_____<br><br>_____<br><br>_____<br><br>_____ |

Let the egg stay in the vinegar overnight and then describe what happens to the shell. _____

_____

How is this like what happens in a cave made of limestone? _____

_____

_____

# Cave Foundations

The children and Ms. Frizzle discovered strange shapes growing from the floor and ceiling of the cave. Those on the ceiling are called *stalactites. Stalagmites* grow up from the floor. These are easy to remember if you think that stalactites must hold "tight" to hang from the ceiling, and stalagmites must be "mighty" strong to grow up from the floor. These beautiful formations are created by water dripping into the cave. As this water evaporates, it leaves deposits of the minerals dissolved in it, which gradually harden into rock. These formations may be white, brown, red, or multicolored, depending on the minerals dissolved in the dripping water.

If the water flows over walls and floors, it leaves a thin film of minerals. This is called *flowstone.* Hanging deposits called *draperies* may also form from thin sheets of minerals building up gradually from the ceiling. These may be so thin that light will shine through them. Sometimes, the formations are hollow so that they make a sound when they are tapped lightly. Commercial tours of caves show people the beauty of these formations.

**To the Students:** Do a simple experiment to simulate the formation of stalactites and flowstone, using a chemical dissolved in water.

**Materials:** magnesium sulfate (Epsom salts), thick cotton string, three small waxed cups, hot water, aluminum pie pan, food coloring (optional)

**Procedure:** Poke a small hole in the center of the bottom of one cup. Gently pull the string through the hole with a hook. The string should plug up the hole but not be squeezed so that the water can slowly drip out of the cup along the string. Wet the string which hangs below the cup thoroughly with water.

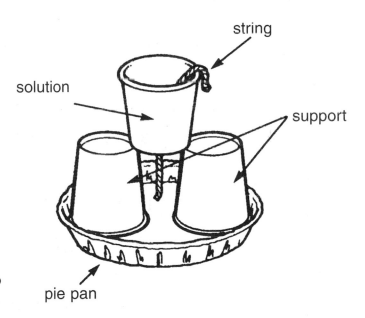

Fill another cup with very hot water, pour in magnesium sulfate, and stir until no more will dissolve. Add a color to the solution, if you wish, to simulate a mineral color. Set the cup with the string in the center of the pie pan, supported by the other two cups so that the string is about ¹/₂ inches (4 cm) above it. Pour the supersaturated solution into the cup with the string. Place the pie pan where it can remain undisturbed for several days.

Make drawings of what happens during the first hour and then over two or thee days. After two days you should see crystals beginning to form in the pie pan. This represents the flowstone. Crystals which form on the string are like stalactites.

# Making a Cave

**To the Teacher:** This activity lets students create a cave diorama to depict what the interior of a cave looks like. It will be helpful to provide a variety of resources which describe caves, including books, pictures, and a video or film of cave exploration (see "Related Books and Periodicals," page 44). If possible, invite someone to speak to the class who has been through caves and can share his or her experiences.

**To the Students:** Review "Cave Facts" (page 13) to understand how caves are formed and look at the information on page 17 to help you understand what a cave looks like inside.

---

## Internet Extender

**Activity:** Visit Lechuguilla Cave, which holds the record for being the deepest cave in the United States. It is only about five miles from the Carlsbad Caverns National Park in New Mexico. The cave is a winding, twisting underground maze which has yet to be completely explored and mapped. Currently, 97.8 miles of Lechuguilla have been explored and mapped, with no end in sight. So far, the deepest part of the cave measured goes down 1,571 feet!

Project the images from these Web sites onto a large monitor so all students can view it at the same time. Begin by scanning down to go on the virtual tour of Lechuguilla Cave. This tour should help students make their own shoebox cave.

**Virtual Tour:** *http://www.extremescience.com/LechuguillaCave.htm*

Click on the circles superimposed on the cave route to see pictures of formations in that area which students can match to the cave formations shown on page 17.

**Cave Photographs:** *http://www.europa.com/~gp/lech/photolist.htm*

These photos can be viewed by clicking on the name of each photo on this Web page.

---

**Materials:** shoe box, colored paper, pieces of Styrofoam, scissors, glue, pictures of caves, marking pens, and any other items which will help create a diorama of a cave's interior

**Procedure:** Now it is your turn to create a cave. Gather the materials, pictures, and information you will need to make a three-dimensional view of the inside of a cave in the shoebox. Try to show examples of cave formations such as stalactites, stalagmites, draperies, flowstone, and columns. You may want to include people or animals in your diorama. You may even create a cave which was used thousands of years ago by the early people who made paintings on the walls.

# Making a Cave *(cont.)*

**To the Teacher:** Make a copy of this page for each student to look at while he/she is creating a shoe box cave. To save paper, you may wish to make a single transparency of this diagram and project it for the students to look at while working on their projects.

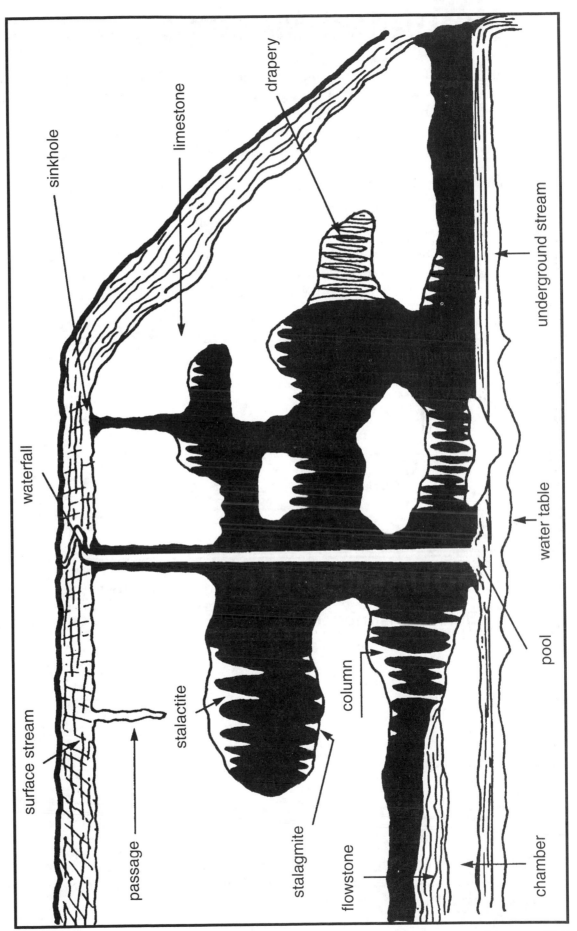

# Simulated Metamorphic Rocks

Ms. Frizzle's class went further into the earth's crust where it was much hotter due to the pressure of the crustal layers above them. They found *metamorphic* rocks, which are rocks that change, as written in Dorothy Ann's report, "Another Earth Science Word." For example, The Friz showed her students marble, which is really limestone that has been changed over millions of years due to pressure and heat. They also discovered slate, the metamorphic form o shale.

Make simulated metamorphic rocks by following the directions below.

**Materials:** seven or eight small marshmallows, wax paper

**Procedure:** Fold a piece of wax paper in half. Place the small marshmallows close together on one half of the paper. Fold the other half over the marshmallows and place this on the floor or a hard surface. Put both of your heels over the wax paper sandwich and gently shift your weight from one foot to the other.

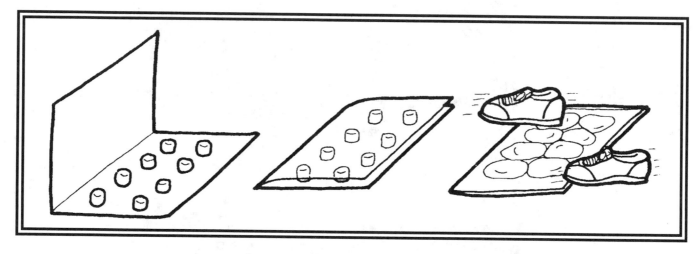

**Closure:** Compare the marshmallows before and after you have added pressure to them.

**Before Description**                                          **After Description**

_____                                _____

_____                                _____

_____                                _____

_____                                _____

_____                                _____

This is similar to metamorphic rock, which is rock that has been changed from being under pressure and heat. This can happen when rock is squeezed and heated as igneous rock, in its molten state, is forced between rock layers.

# Simulated Igneous Rocks

Going even farther toward the center of the earth, the class found *igneous* rock, which is formed when rock becomes so hot that it melts and is forced through cracks in the earth's crust. It then cools and turns into rock. Try an experiment to see how a solid can be melted to liquid and then cooled to a solid state again.

**To the Teacher:** The students will need assistance with this activity since it requires heating sugar over a hot plate. The recipe will make peanut brittle; you may substitute other nuts if you prefer.

**Materials:** one cup (250 mL) of sugar, a frying pan, aluminum pie pan, butter, peanuts, hot plate, spoon, tall clear glass filled with water

**Procedure:** Grease the aluminum pie pan with the butter. Place the nuts in the pie pan to simulate rocks. Pretend the sugar is sedimentary or metamorphic rock. Pour it into the frying pan and heat it over the hot plate. Watch the sugar as it is heated and notice that it begins to melt. Stir it until all of the sugar is melted. Pour most of it into the aluminum pie pan, saving about two tablespoons (30 mL) of the liquid. Slowly pour the remaining liquid into the water. Complete the chart by recording your observations immediately after the activity and during the following 15 minutes as the brittle takes on its final form.

## Making Igneous Rocks

What happened as the sugar was heated? _____

| Describe what happened when the melted sugar was poured into the pie pan. | Describe what happened when the melted sugar was poured into the water. |
|---|---|
| _____ <br><br> _____ | _____ <br><br> _____ |
| Draw what happened and label your drawing: | Draw what happened and label your drawing: |
| Compare this to lava pouring down the sides of a volcano. <br><br> _____ <br><br> _____ <br><br> _____ | Compare this to lava pouring into the ocean. <br><br> _____ <br><br> _____ <br><br> _____ |

# Earth's Layers

After the bus had dug through the earth's crust, it got hotter and hotter as it zoomed toward the center of the earth. The crust is about five miles (eight km) thick below the ocean to about 25 miles (40 km) thick below the continents. In 1961, American scientists began "Project Mohole," which was an attempt to drill through the earth's crust and into the mantle. They began drilling from a ship into the floor of the Pacific Ocean. It became too expensive to continue this project, however, so they had to stop before even getting near the mantle layer. The deepest borehole reaches 7.5 miles (12 km) beneath Russia's Kola Peninsula, still far above the mantle.

## Earth Facts

The earth is about 7,928 miles (12,685 km) in diameter. Most scientists believe the earth is divided into five layers. The inside view of the earth shown on the next page gives information about these layers. The thinnest part of the crust is beneath the ocean; the thickest is beneath the continents.

Scientists know what the interior of the earth must be like from studying earthquake data. They measure how fast and in what directions earthquake waves travel through the earth. The temperature and density of the material inside the earth can be calculated from this information. The mantle/core boundary is a division between the mantle and core. It varies in thickness as it is pulled and pushed by the lower mantle, moving in a swirling pattern caused by convection currents.

It may seem strange that the inner core of the earth is the hottest part, but the iron and nickel are solid, not melted as in the outer core. The pressure of the rest of the earth on the inner core is so great that the molecules of the iron and nickel are packed so tightly they form solid crystals.

---

## Internet Extender

**To the Teacher:** If a large monitor is available, use it to project the images from these Web sites so that students can view and discuss them.

**Activity:** See what the earth's crust looks like and learn where the tectonics plates are.

**Our Dynamic Earth** http://www.nasm.si.edu/earthtoday/dynam.htm

**Note:** There are many graphics at this Web site which take a while to download.

• Scroll down to view of the earth and click on geosphere.

• Read the information for each view of earth and then click on the related image to see it in more detail.

**Activity:** View the interior of the earth and learn about its layers.

**Earth's Interior and Plate Tectonics** http://spaceart.com/solar/eng/earthint.htm

• Click on the graphic of the cutaway view of the earth. Scroll down to read how scientists know what the interior of earth looks like, as well as what the thickness of the layers are. Scroll up to options and click on earthint.jpg (463K) to see an enlarged, more detailed version of this graphic. Point out how thin the earth's crust is compared to its interior layers.

• Go back to the previous page and scroll down to examine the information about the earth's interior. Click on the graphic of the divisions in the earth's interior to see a larger image for more details.

• Read and discuss the descriptions of the layers within the earth.

---

# Earth's Layers *(cont.)*

**To the Teacher:** Use a transparency of this diagram, along with the information on page 20, to teach about the inside of the earth.

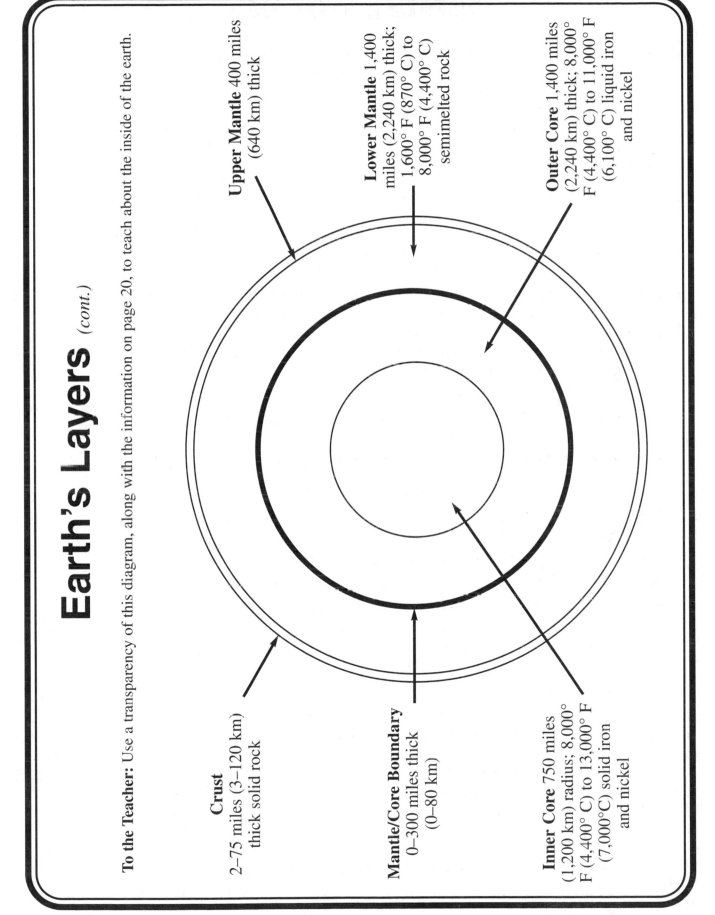

**Upper Mantle** 400 miles (640 km) thick

**Lower Mantle** 1,400 miles (2,240 km) thick; 1,600° F (870° C) to 8,000° F (4,400° C) semimelted rock

**Outer Core** 1,400 miles (2,240 km) thick; 8,000° F (4,400° C) to 11,000° F (6,100° C) liquid iron and nickel

**Crust** 2–75 miles (3–120 km) thick solid rock

**Mantle/Core Boundary** 0–300 miles thick (0–80 km)

**Inner Core** 750 miles (1,200 km) radius; 8,000° F (4,400° C) to 13,000° F (7,000°C) solid iron and nickel

# Earth Model

Turn a Styrofoam ball into a model of the earth. This will help you understand the thickness of the different layers of our planet.

**Materials:** 3-inch (7.5 cm) Styrofoam ball; blue, yellow, red, brown, and orange watercolor markers; fine-point black felt-tip pen; page 23; straight pins; scissors

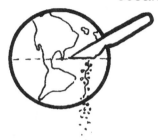

Use the end of the strip to make an equator.

**Procedure:** Make a strip of paper ¹/₂ inch (1.3 cm) wide and 4.7 inches (11.8 cm) long and then fold it in half to find the middle. Place the strip on the Styrofoam ball and put a pin through its middle fold line to hold it in place. Use the black marker to draw a mark at the end of the strip. Keeping it pinned in the same place, swivel the strip around the ball slightly and make another mark with the pen. Repeat this around the ball, marking a dotted line. Connect the dots to form an equator.

Draw the continents and color the ocean blue.

Cut along the equator.

Use a felt-tip pen to draw a rough outline of each continent on the ball (globe). Look at a copy of page 23 to see where the continents should fit relative to each other and to the equator. On your globe, add blue around the continents to represent the ocean.

Place the ball on newspaper and ask your teacher to carefully use a serrated knife to cut it in half at the equator. Now, you are ready to make a model of the inside of the earth.

Cut out the circle of the earth drawing on the right. Cut along the dotted line and then cut the layers apart. Pin the circles to the inside of one of the halves of the ball. Do not pin the inner core circle to the ball. Color the inner core area brown. Place the inner core circle over the area you just colored and remove the outer core circle. Color the area of the outer core orange. Next outline the outside edge of the outer core with a black pen to show the mantle/core boundary. Cover the orange area with the outer core circle and remove the lower mantle circle. Color this area red and then cover it with the lower mantle circle. Remove the upper mantle circle and paint this area yellow. The crust of the earth is so thin that it is represented by the thin layer of blue on the outside of the ball.

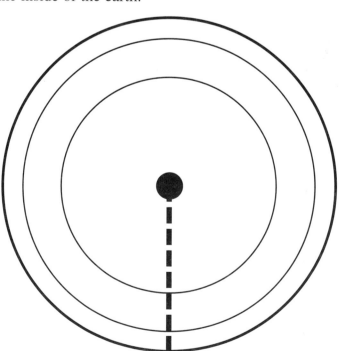

Cut out the outermost circle and then cut along the dotted line.

**Closure:** Use your model to complete the "Layers of the Earth" chart on page 25.

# Earth Model *(cont.)*

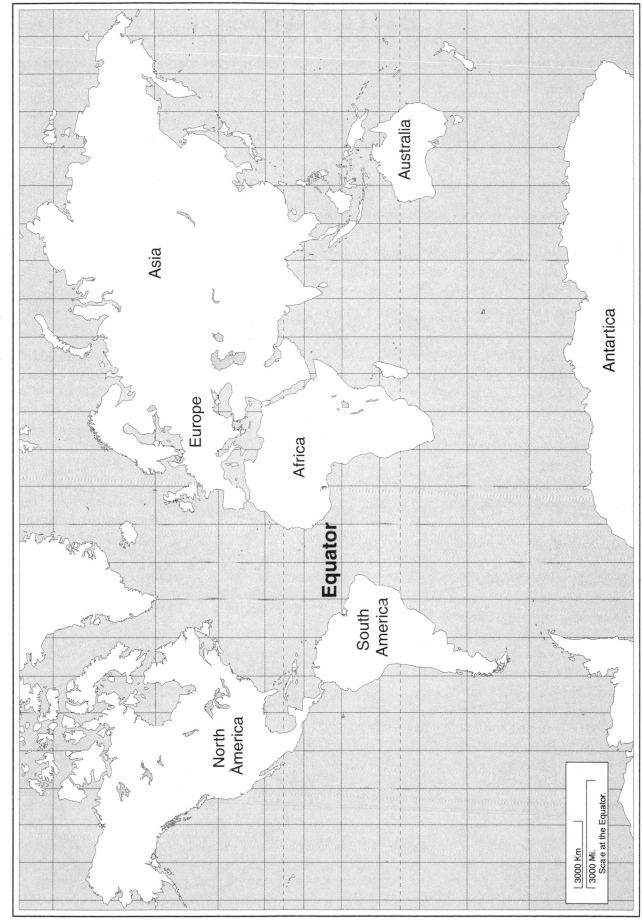

Australia

Asia

Europe

Africa

Antartica

Equator

South America

North America

3000 Km
3000 Mi.
Scale at the Equator.

# Earth Model *(cont.)*

Scientists think that when the earth first formed, it was a ball of gas spun off from the sun. Gradually the gas cooled, but as it cooled the more dense material moved into the center of the earth. The tremendous pressure of the layers of the earth creates the heat which keeps the rock beneath the crust in a semimelted or melted state. Only the inner core is solid, like the crust, since the molecules in its iron and nickel are held tightly, packed by the pressure of the layers above.

Add these flags to your earth model to label the layers of the earth.

**Materials:** flags, five straight pins

**Procedure:** Complete the information on the five flags below by writing in the thickness of cach laycr. The thickness of the crust has been done for you as an example. Anchor the flags to the sections on the inside of the ball, which have been colored to represent the different layers. Do this by weaving a straight pin through the end of the triangle and then sticking it into the layer it describes. (See the illustration.)

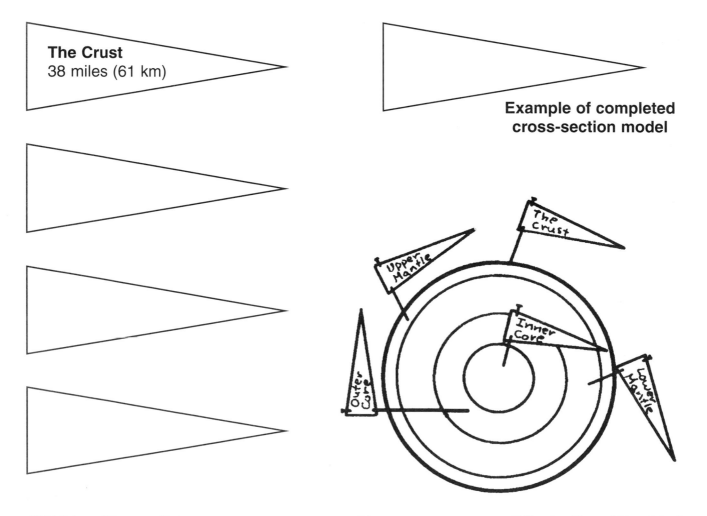

**The Crust**
38 miles (61 km)

**Example of completed
cross-section model**

# Earth Model *(cont.)*

The earth is about 8,000 miles (12,800 km) in diameter, which means the radius (distance to the center) is about 4,000 miles (6,400 km). Use this information to calculate the percent each layer is of the entire earth. First, estimate what you think this percentage (%) is for a layer and then record the layer's thickness and divide it by the radius.

> The layer's thickness ÷ 4,000 mi (6,400 km = percentage of the total earth.

The crust layer has been done for you.

## LAYERS OF THE EARTH

| Layer | Estimated Percentage of the Total Earth | Thickness | Actual Percentage of the Total Earth |
|---|---|---|---|
| **Crust** | 5% | 38 miles (61km) (average) | 1% (rounded off) |
| **Upper Mantle** | | 400 miles (640 km) | |
| **Lower Mantle** | | 1,400 miles (2,240 km) | |
| **Outer Core** | | 1,400 miles (2,240 km) | |
| **Inner Core** | | 750 miles (1,200 km) radius | |

1. How did the estimate of the crust's percentage of the total earth compare with the actual calculations of it?_____

    _____

    _____

2. How did the estimates you made for each of the other layers compare with the actual answers?

    _____

    _____

3. How does the thickness of the crust compare to the other layers of the earth? _____

    _____

    _____

# Cracked Crust

Alfred Wegener, a German meteorologist and geophysicist, proposed a theory in 1912 that the continents were once all together and then were slowly forced apart to where they are today. People laughed at him, but after his death, scientists proved he was absolutely right.

## Earth Facts

Look at the model you made of the earth. Remember that the earth's crust is only a thin covering over the rest of the planet. Since Alfred Wegener's time, a great deal has been learned about the earth's crust and interior. Scientists have discovered a ridge running roughly north to south down the middle of the Atlantic Ocean floor. They took samples of the rocks on either side of this ridge and used special instruments to find how old they are. What these measurements told them was surprising. The rocks near the top of the ridge are younger than those found further down the sides of the ridge. In fact, the rocks continue to get older as you move east or west from the ridge toward the edge of the continents which border the Atlantic Ocean.

Deep sea diving devices help scientists see what is happening far below the ocean's surface. They have been able to observe melted rock (lava) pouring from cracks in the ocean floor, like toothpaste forced from a tube. This lava is magma, leaking from the upper mantle and forcing sections of the crust apart. Earthquakes and volcanoes occur along the edges of the continents circling the Pacific Ocean. Volcanoes also are found in the middle of this ocean.

What can explain all of this? Scientists think the earth's crust is cracked like an eggshell. The crust is pushed by new material being forced out of the upper layer of the mantle. The continents and ocean floor ride on large pieces of the crust, called plates. Sometimes these plates are pushed together, and one may slide under the other. When this happens, the nearby area has an earthquake. California and Japan are on plates which cause many earthquakes.

**Activity:** Learn about plate tectonics.

- Make a transparency of the map on page 27 and show it to the students. Have them look at South America and Africa. Ask them if these continents look like puzzle pieces which should fit together. Point out the cracks which extend around the crust, outlining eight large areas. Show the arrows which indicate the direction these crustal plates are moving.

---

## Internet Extender

**To the Teacher:** If a large monitor is available, use it to project the images from these Web sites so that students can view and discuss them.

**Activity:** View an animation of continental drift from 750 million years ago to the present.

**Plate Tectonics**

*http://www.ucmp.berkeley.edu/geology/tectonics.html*

- Look at the drawing showing the crustal plates and read the brief information about this.
- Scroll down and click on <u>history</u> to learn about the early theory of continental drift.
- Go back to the previous page and then click on <u>mechanism</u> to get the latest information on what moves these plates.
- Scroll down to select the first animation (this loads faster than the others). Have students watch the continents move over these millions of years. Stop the animation at various intervals to discuss the position of the continents and compare them with a world map.

---

# Cracked Earth Map

Most earthquakes occur near or along the boundaries of the rocky plates of the earth's crust. Each dot on this map shows where a major earthquake has occurred during the past 30 years. The arrows indicate the directions of the plates' movements.

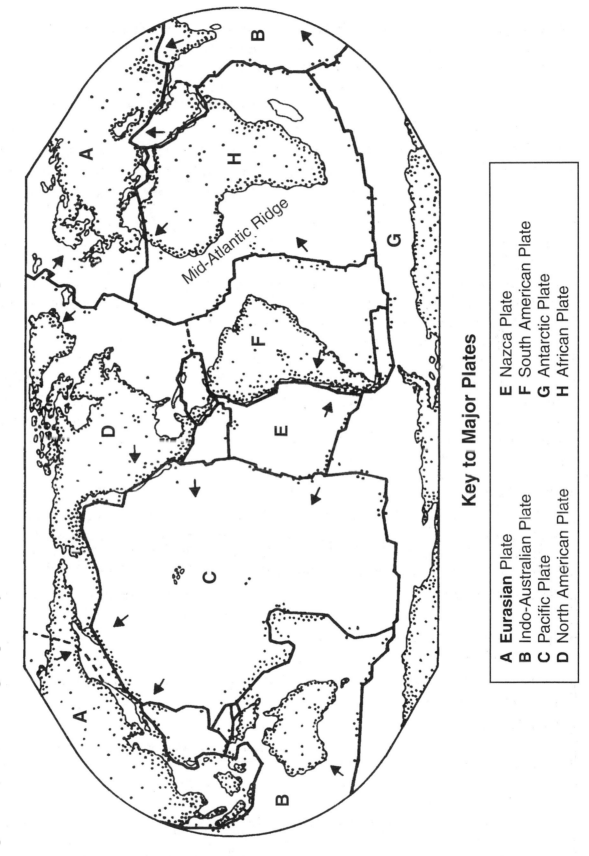

## Key to Major Plates

**A** Eurasian Plate      **E** Nazca Plate
**B** Indo-Australian Plate      **F** South American Plate
**C** Pacific Plate      **G** Antarctic Plate
**D** North American Plate      **H** African Plate

# Why Does the Crust Move?

Although scientists cannot get under the earth's crust to look at it, they can tell what the earth's layers are like by examining earthquake data. When an earthquake happens, it gives off shock waves. These shock waves travel across the crust, as well as deep into the earth. The waves move at different rates of speed, faster through a solid than a liquid and faster through colder layers than warmer ones. This has helped scientists decide what the temperatures of the layers beneath the earth's crust are and if the material is solid, liquid, or semiliquid.

A simple demonstration can explain how the mantle can push the crust of the earth around. It uses the principle of convection currents to explain this. We see convection currents at work on the surface of the earth. Warm gases or liquids rise, and cold gases or liquids sink. This is observed in the atmosphere and in bodies of water.

Do a simple experiment, using drops of hot and cold water to see how they react when dropped into room temperature water.

**Materials:** clear plastic cup, very hot water, ice cold water, room temperature water, two droppers, red and blue food coloring, two small Styrofoam cups

**Procedure:** Fill the clear plastic cup with water and let it sit for about 10 minutes so that the temperature will be the same as the classroom. Carefully fill one of the Styroform cups about a quarter full of hot water and color it dark red. Put ice water into the other Styroform cup until it is also about a quarter full and color it dark blue. Use one of the droppers to put a few drops of cold water into the water in the plastic cup. Use the other dropper to put a few drops of hot water into the same cup. Record what happens below.

| Water Temperature Experiment | | |
| --- | --- | --- |
| Add drops of water to the room temperature water and then complete the chart. | | |
| | **Tell What Happened** | **Draw What Happened** |
| **Cold Water** | | |
| **Hot Water** | | |

What does this experiment tell you about how the magma in the earth's mantle behaves when it is heated by the outer core or cools as it comes in contact with the undersurface of the crust? (Answer on the back of this page.)

# Why Does the Crust Move? *(cont.)*

**To the Teacher:** Do the following demonstration to show your students how convection currents work and then compare this with the motion of the magma in the mantle beneath the earth's crust

**Materials:** large glass bread dish (oven safe), aquarium heater, ice, small plastic bag, red and blue food coloring, water, masking tape

**Procedure:** Place the glass bread dish on books on a table so that the students will be able to see it clearly. Fill the glass bread dish with water within about one inch (2.5 cm) from the top. Put the aquarium heater at one end and tape it in place. Plug it in and turn it to the highest setting to warm the water. After the water feels warm to the touch (about 5-8 minutes), gather the students around the table. Place them so that they will be looking through the sides of the dish, not down on it. Place a plastic bag with several ice cubes inside at the opposite end of the dish from the heater and tape it in place. Explain to the students that this represents the layers of the earth with the heater being the core of the earth and heating the mantle (water) and the ice representing the cooler undersurface of the crust. Tell them that you will be using red; and blue food coloring to trace the different temperatures of water; red will represent the hot water and blue, the cold water.

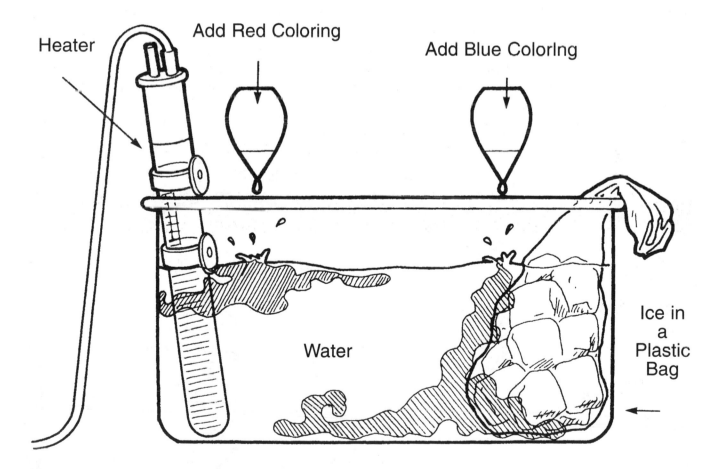

Heater     Add Red Coloring     Add Blue Coloring

Water     Ice in a Plastic Bag

**Glass Bread Dish**

# Why Does the Crust Move? *(cont.)*

Ask the students to think back to their experiment with hot and cold water and have them predict what will happen when you put a drop of red food coloring in the water near the heater. Do this and have the students watch the food coloring stay on the surface and begin to spread across the water. Next, ask them to predict what will happen when blue coloring is added near the ice. Place one drop of blue coloring near the ice and let the students see that it immediately sinks and begins to spread across the bottom. Compare this to what happens in the earth. Crustal material which is forced back into the mantle is colder, therefore denser, and sinks. Eventually, the material in the mantle reaches the hotter outer core and begins to heat up, becoming less dense and, therefore, rising to the surface. At this point continue to watch the colored water and point out that when the red reaches the ice cold area it begins to sink, while the blue moves across the bottom and eventually reaches the heater, where it becomes warmer and starts to rise. This continues as long as there are the two extremes of temperature setting up a convection current, acting much like a conveyor belt at the checkout stand in the supermarket.

**Closure:** Make a transparency of the drawing "Convection Currents Move the Crust" on the next page Color the picture, making the ocean blue and the continent green. Color the material being subducted dark blue and the arrows showing the rising mantle material red. Hot spots should be colored yellow, since this material is hotter than the rest of the mantle. Color the inner core brown and the area of the outer core orange-red. Use the drawing and the "Explanation of the Terms" (page 32) to help explain to the students how scientists think convection currents are created and how they move the earth's crust.

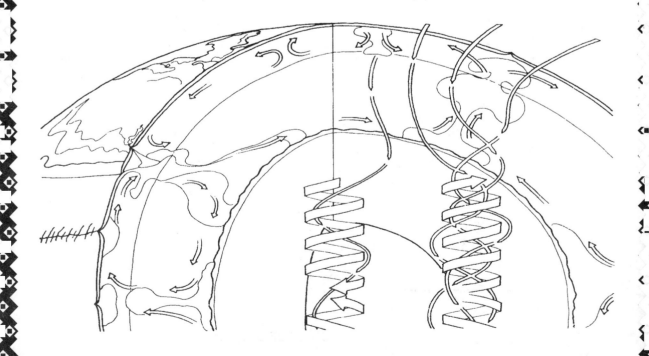

# Convection Currents Move the Crust

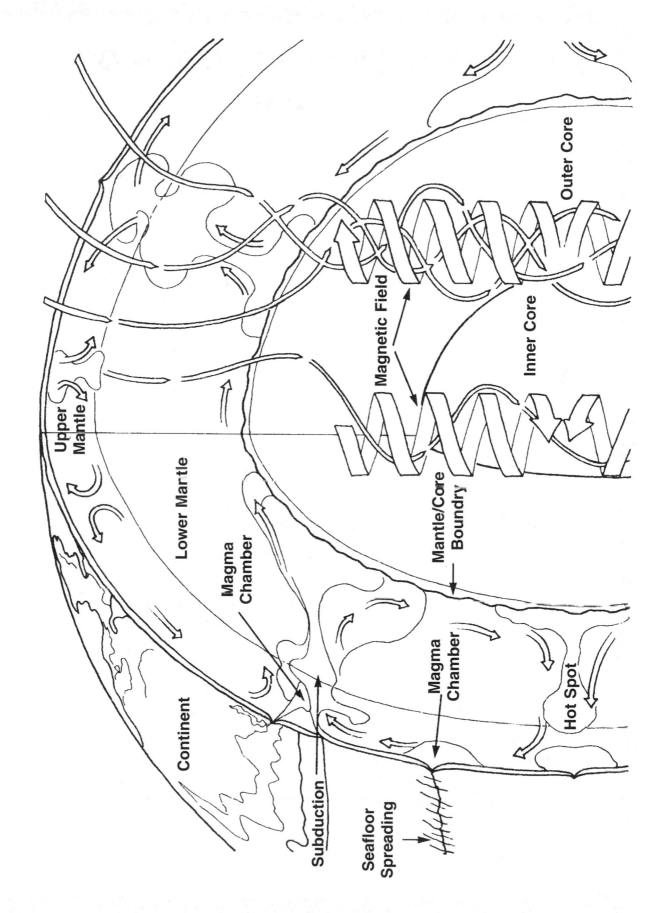

Upper Mantle

Lower Mantle

Magma Chamber

Continent

Subduction

Seafloor Spreading

Magma Chamber

Hot Spot

Mantle/Core Boundry

Magnetic Field

Inner Core

Outer Core

# Convection Currents Move the Crust *(cont.)*

## Explanation of the Terms

**Continents:** Continents are made of lighter rock than seafloors, and so they rarely dive into the mantle. A collision between continental plates forms a mountain range, such as those running north-south in California.

**Hot Spots:** A plume of hot rock melts and rises like a fountain from deep in the mantle. When it reaches the crust, it forces through it, forming a volcano. As the crust moves along above the mantle, the plume makes a chain of volcanoes, leaving behind the old, dead volcano cones. This is how the Hawaiian Islands were created and are still being formed today.

**Inner Core:** This area is still a mystery, but most scientists believe it is solid iron and nickel. It is growing as the outer core continues to turn into a solid.

**Magma Chamber:** Magma rises and melts large pockets or chambers in the surrounding rock, as close as two miles (3 km) to the surface. More magma rises in the chamber, building a reservoir from which volcanic materials erupt.

**Mantle:** Material heated by the core rises to take the place of the cooler rock which is sinking. The sinking rock warms as it nears the core and rises again. This happens continuously, creating convection currents which move the crustal plates above the mantle. The mantle is divided into an upper and lower layer.

**Mantle/Core Boundary:** Mantle magma meets the semiliquid metal in the outer core. The thickness of this boundary ranges from near nothing to several hundred miles.

**Outer Core:** The motion from convection currents and the earth's spin of rotation cause material in the outer core to move in spirals parallel to the north-south axis of the earth. The spiral motion of the material generates electricity, forming something like an electromagnet and creating the earth's magnetic field.

**Seafloor Spreading:** As two plates beneath the oceans pull apart at mid-ocean ridges, the magma in the mantle rises to fill the gap and hardens. Magma continues to be added to the plates as they drift apart.

**Subduction:** When two plates push together, one usually dives under the other. The leading edge of the plate melts as it meets the hot mantle and then begins to plunge deeper into the mantle. If lava is released, volcanoes occur in the crust. The force of one plate against the other results in earthquakes. This is happening in California, since the state is split between the Pacific Plate and the North American Plate. These plates are moving in different directions (see the "Cracked Earth Map" on page 27).

# Inside a Volcano

The students were really glad when Ms. Frizzle headed the bus out of the earth's center. They reached the crust and drove through a tunnel of black rock. The tunnel led to the surface of the crust through a volcano which was an island. The class got out of the bus and discovered igneous rocks ot basalt and obsidian and floating rocks called pumice. Suddenly, they heard a rumbling noise! They hurried back into the bus just in time as the volcano began to erupt, pouring out lava which shot into the air and flowed into the ocean. The lava was so hot it made the water near the shore begin to boil, raising a cloud of steam. The bus sprouted a parachute and began to rise on the cloud.

**To the Teacher:** Make a copy of the picture below to show students the cross section of a volcano. Share the information in "How Volcanoes Form" with the students.

## How Volcanoes Form

Volcanoes begin when magma from the mantle melts a pocket (chamber) into the crust. Pressure from gas and heat eventually forces the magma up from the chamber through a weak area in the crust. The gas and magma (now called lava) blast out of a central opening or vent which is at the top of the volcano. Most of the lava then erupts through the vent, piling up around this opening. Layers from many eruptions build up to form a volcanic mountain or volcano.

Not all of the magma reaches the surface through the central vent. Some may flow through the side vents in the volcano or remain below the surface. Magma may also force its way through cracks in the volcano and cool before reaching the surface. This hardens into igneous rock.

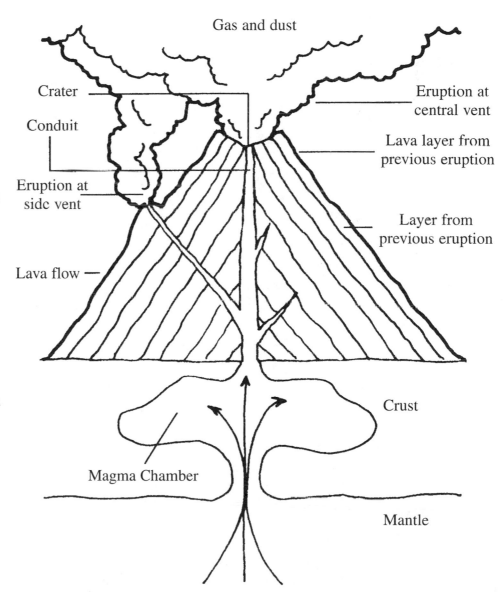

# Volcano Simulation

**To the Students:** You can make a simple demonstration to show how magma flows from a volcano.

**Materials:** clear long-necked plastic bottle (e.g., salad dressing or syrup bottle), funnel, clear vinegar, red food coloring, a deep pan (or a sink), tablespoon, measuring cup with a spout, baking soda

**Procedure:** Pour about three tablespoons (45 mL) of baking soda into the bottle through the funnel. Pour about ¼ cup (62.5 mL) of vinegar into the measuring cup and add coloring to make it dark red. Place the bottle into the deep pan or sink (this is a messy experiment), pour the vinegar into the bottle without using the funnel, and then watch the reaction closely.

On another piece of paper, describe and draw what happened after you added vinegar. Label your drawing to show how this is like a volcano. Use the terms *volcano, central vent, magma chamber, lava, gas.*

---

### Internet Extender

**Activity:** View a picture history of the Kilauea Volcano in Hawaii. If a large screen computer monitor is available, use it for the entire class to do this activity together.

**Images of Volcanoes**

*http://volcano.und.nodak.edu/vwdocs/volc_images/volc_images.html*

- Click on North American section (upper right) of the world map.
- Click on the box over Hawaiian Islands in Pacific Ocean (lower left).
- Locate the big island of Hawaii on this map and click on it.
- Study the map of Hawaii and find the Kilauea Volcano, one of the most active volcanoes on earth, and then click on it. Use the following questions to lead a discussion of the information given.

    1. When was the present Kilauea Caldera formed? (1790)

    2. What is a *caldera*? Click on the word to see its meaning in the glossary. (*Caldera* is the Spanish word for caldron, a basin-shaped volcanic depression—by definition, at least one mile in diameter.)

    3. How many years ago did the current eruption begin? (It began in 1983.)

- Use the pull-down screen under "Select a Page to Jump to."

    1. 3D of Kilauea—The teacher reads the text and simplifies it for students as needed.

    2. Map of recent flows—Use the scale to measure perimeter of the flows (22.5 miles).

    3. 1996 Eruption—View the picture, read, and discuss the description.

    4. Wahaula Heiau destruction—Use Quick Time version for sound and enlarge the picture by pulling on the lower right corner before viewing.

Click on <u>Kilauea ERZ-USGS Open File</u> (includes scenes and sounds of hot lava, lava flows and fountains, and lava entering water).

Click on <u>Eruption of Kilauea 1959–1960</u> (includes scenes and sounds of collecting samples, building of main crater, large gas bubble rising, fountain at night, and lava colors).

---

# Comparing Famous Volcanoes

There are many famous volcanoes found on earth. Some of these are listed on the chart below. Find information about these volcanoes and complete the chart.

## Famous Volcanoes

| Name | Location | Height | Interesting Facts |
|---|---|---|---|
| **Mount St. Helens** | Washington, U.S.A. | 8,364 feet (2,549 m) | eruped in 1980 with a blast of molten rock and hot ash which flattened forest, melted snow, and caused floods |
| **Krakatoa** | | | |
| **Kilauea** | | | |
| **Vesuvius** | | | |
| **Paricutin** | | | |
| **Stromoli** | | | |

**Closure:** Add these volcanoes to the earth model you have made. Find the exact location of each of the volcanoes in an atlas. Use straight pins with large heads to represent the volcanoes and put them on the model in their correct locations. Notice how many of these are right on the edge of a plate. Kilauea, a volcano on the big island of Hawaii, is an exception because it sits in the middle of the Pacific Plate and is caused by a hot spot of magma pushing up from the mantle.

# Recycling Rocks

**To the Teacher:** Enlarge the drawing of "Recycling the Earth's Crust" (page 37) onto a large piece of butcher paper or bed sheet so that students will be able to walk on it. (Here is the easiest way to make an enlargement of the diagram Tape the butcher paper to the wall. Make a transparency of the diagram and project it onto the paper. Outline the projection with a black marker.) You may want to use colored pens to show different rock layers and temperatures. Add the labels to the large drawing. The script below should be read aloud as students take turns walking through the rock cycle.

## Walking Through the Rock Cycle

1. Begin your journey beneath the earth's crust in a magma chamber just below the floor of the ocean. The magma is semiliquid since temperatures are at least 1,600° F (870° C). The magma is under tremendous pressure from convection currents, which pushes itthrough cracks in the ocean floor (like toothpaste heing squeezed from a tube). It is nowcalled lava.

2. Once it breaks through the crust, it is lava. As the lava mixes with the cooler ocean water, it turns into igneous rock, adding to the top and the sides of the crustal plate.

3. This plate also has sedimentary rock created by shells falling to the floor of the ocean and piling up until the pressure of their weight squeezes them into rock layers. Beneath the sedimentary rock is metamorphic rock, made when sedimentary rock is heated due to pressure and when it gets near igneous rock.

4. The plate continues to be forced apart as more lava rises through the crack. It is carried along like a giant conveyor belt by the convection currents in the magma located in the upper mantle just underneath the crust. The edge of the plate is pushed up against another one and is forced to dive beneath it.

5. The leading edge of the plate begins to melt as it mixes with the hotter magma. This new material is heavy and starts to sink, only to become so hot that it rises again in another area under the continental plate.

6. Another magma chamber is formed and forces lava up the central vent of a volcano.

7. The force of the lava creates a volcano which gives off clouds of gas and fountains of lava.

8. The lava runs down the side of the volcano. Some lava cools into igneous rock, while the rest continues to the ocean where it cools quickly as it hits the water.

9. Great clouds of steam rise as the lava cools quickly, creating tiny fragments of igneous rock. The waves eventually break the fragments into smaller and smaller pieces which become black sand.

10. Some of the black sand washes to the ocean floor, piling up and making a new layer of sediment which gradually becomes rock from the pressure of the new layers of sand.

The rocks in the earth's crust are constantly being recycled like this. All of the minerals on earth have been here since it began, which most scientists believe is about 4.5 billion years ago. The continuous change of these rocks is called the *rock cycle*.

# Recycling the Earth's Crust

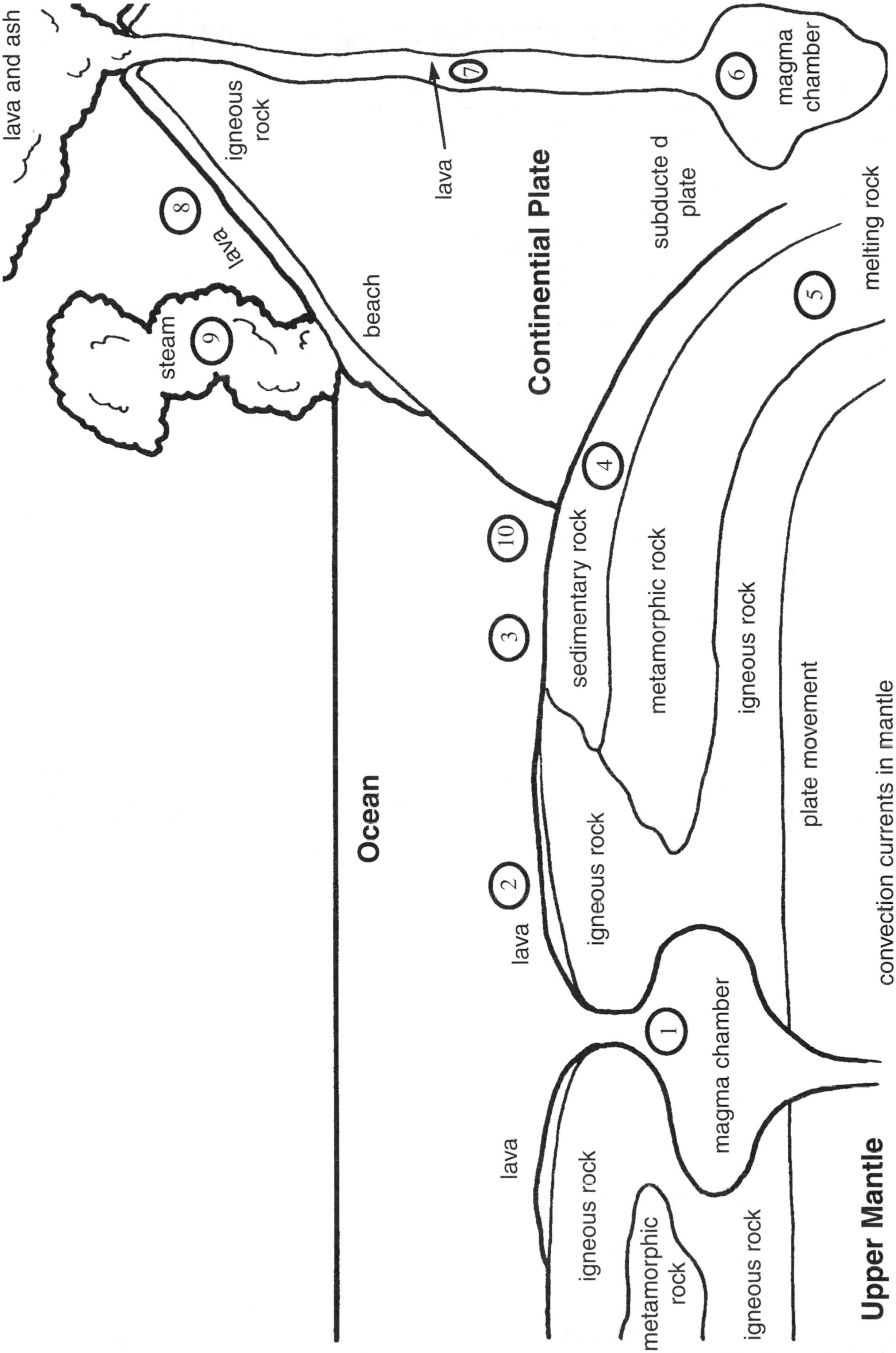

lava and ash

igneous rock

lava

magma chamber

7

6

Continental Plate

subducte d plate

melting rock

5

8

lava

beach

steam

9

sedimentary rock

metamorphic rock

igneous rock

10

4

Ocean

3

igneous rock

plate movement

convection currents in mantle

2

lava

magma chamber

1

lava

igneous rock

metamorphic rock

igneous rock

Upper Mantle

# Identifying Minerals

When Ms. Frizzle and the students returned from their trip, they made a display of the rocks they had collected. They identified the rocks by mineral and type (i.e., sedimentary), and they told how the rocks can be used.

**To the Teacher:** Students will make a display of their rock specimens in this activity. Introduce or review Mohs' Hardness Scale (see page 8) prior to assigning the activity. You may wish to display the hardness standards in a prominent location as students complete the chart. You may want to purchase sets of minerals to provide students with a wider variety of specimens and the opportunity to learn how to identify them. Delta Education, Inc., (see "Related Materials," page 45) supplies relatively inexpensive sets of the rninerals listed on the chart through their *Elementary Science Study* (ESS) catalog. The students will need easy guides for mineral identification. These can 'ne found in bookstores and science shops. Also, check the "Related Books and Periodicals" section on page 44 for suggestions.

**To the Students:** Use the rocks you brought to school at the beginning of this unit to create a classroom display. Follow the techniques you used to describe your rock in the "Can You Find My Mineral?" activity (page 8) and the chart below to help you identify your rocks.

**Materials:** mineral samples, penny, steel nail, unglazed tile, mineral identification books, a copy of the "Mineral Identification Key" (page 39).

**Procedure:** Complete the chart below to describe your mineral(s) and then match the description with the "Mineral Identification Key." If your mineral does not fit any of these descriptions, look for it in a mineral identification book.

## My Mineral Identification Chart

| Color | Luster | Texture | Streak | Hardness | Mineral Name |
|---|---|---|---|---|---|
| | | | | | |
| | | | | | |
| | | | | | |
| | | | | | |

# Mineral Identification Key

Match your minerals to these descriptions and then find their names

| Color | Luster | Texture | Streak | Hardness | Mineral Name |
|-------|--------|---------|--------|----------|--------------|
| calcite | tan and white | shiny and glassy | smooth | white and pink | penny 3 |
| galena | silver | metallic and shiny | smooth to rough | dark gray or black | penny 3 |
| graphite | dark grey | dull | smooth to bumpy | black or dark gray | fingernail 1 |
| quartz | milky white | shiny and glassy | smooth to bumpy | white | none more than 6.5 |
| obsidian | black | glassy | smooth with sharp edges | none | none more than 6.5 |
| hematite | reddish brown | dull | rough | red-brown | fingernail to nail 1-6 |
| magnetite | gray or black | dull | rough | black or dark gray | none above 7 |
| talc | light gray, may have some white | dull | smooth, feels like soap | white | fingernail 1 |

# What Did You Learn?

To the Teacher: Students will draw the inside of the earth and then compare their drawings with the original ones they made in the beginning of the unit (page 4). Students will also write and draw about how they think rocks are made (activity previously done on page 4). The final part of this assessment lets students select one of three questions to answer and illustrate. These activities will assess the depth of conceptual understanding students gained during this study.

**To the Students:** Remember the model of the earth which you made in this unit as you draw a cutaway view of the inside of the earth in the circle below.

### Cutaway View of the Earth

1. Label the layers of the inside of the eartll.

2. Compare this drawing with the one you made before doing the activities in this unit.

3. Write something that you have learned about each of the layers of the earth.

_____

_____

_____

_____

_____

# What Did You Learn? *(cont.)*

Write a brief description of how the earth's rocks are formed. Then make drawings to help explain your description. *Be sure to label your drawings.*

_____

_____

_____

Choose **one** of the following questions to answer. Pretend you are writing this for someone who has not studied this topic. Include a drawing with labels to help him or her understand your answer.

1. What is the rock cycle?

2. How are volcanoes formed?

3. What causes the earth's crust to move?

_____

_____

_____

# Assessment Rubric

Look at all of the papers before awarding any points to gain a feel for how well the students were able to answer the questions. This will determine how strictly to apply this rubric. The rubric scores described below are based on the majority of students understanding the concepts which were taught through thc activities. If the majority of students did not demonstrate a thorough understanding uf the concepts, the activities may have been too difficult for their ability levels. Students should not be penalized by receiving low scores in this case. Adjust the scores to fit the ability level of the majority of the students.

---

### Five-Point Rubric

**4** Student demonstrates a thorough understanding of the concepts.

**3** Student demonstrates a good understanding of the concepts.

**2** Student demonstrates a good understanding of most of the concepts.

**I** Student attempts to answer the questions but obviously does not understand the concepts.

**0** Student does not attempt to answer the questions.

---

### Concepts Covered in This Assessment

The earth consists of layers of different thicknesses and materials as follows:

| Layer | Material | Thickness |
| --- | --- | --- |
| Crust | solid rock | 2–75 miles (3–120 km) |
| Upper Mantle | semimelted rock | 400 miles (640 km) |
| Lower Mantle | semimelted rock | 1,400 miles (2,240 km) |
| Outer Core | liquid iron and nickel | 1,400 miles (2,240 km) |
| Inner Core | liquid iron and nickel | 750 miles (1,000 km) radius |

# Assessment Rubric (cont.)

## Concepts Covered in This Assessment (cont.)

**Layers of the Earth:**

- The crust is so thin that it is only 1% of the earth's diameter.

- The mantle has convection currents created by extremes in temperature which force the crust apart into plates, gradually moving them around.

- A layer of material separates the outer core from the lower mantle.

- The inner core, although extremely hot, is solid due to the pressure of the rest of the layers around it pressing the material into a solid.

- Most scientists believe the earth formed 4.5 billion years ago as a ball of gas spun off the sun. The earth's surface gradually cooled, and the densest material settled in the center.

- Scientists know about the inner layers of the earth from earthquake data.

**How the Three Types of Rocks Are Formed:**

- *Sedimentary rocks* are formed by compacted pieces of rock which were ground down through erosion. When the ground-up rocks fall to the bottom of large bodies of water, they form layers called *sediment*. It can also be made of layers of shells from organisms in the ocean.

- *Igneous rock* is new rock that is formed from melted rock which may have been sedimentary, igneous, or metamorphic rock.

- *Metamorphic rock* is rock that once was sedimentary or igneous but is changed due to heat and pressure deep inside the crust.

**Rock Cycle:** See pages 36 and 37, "Walking Through the Rock Cycle."

**Volcano Formation:** See page 33, "Inside a Volcano."

**Crustal Movement:** See pages 28–32, "Why Does the Crust Move?"

---

### Internet Extender

**Activity:** Look at the Frequently Asked Questions (FAQ) at this Web site. Brainstorm questions which could be asked of geologists that are not found in this section but which students would like answered. Send them to the geologist.

**To the Teacher:** Each question goes to a different USGS earth scientist. Students should receive a reply within a few days. There is no guarantee that a reply is sent for every message. The geologists will not write reports or answer test questions for the students.

**Ask a Geologist**

*USGS http://walrus.wr.usgs.gov/docs/ask-a-ge.html/*

---

# Related Books and Periodicals

Bosak, Susan. Science Is . . . *A Source Book ofFascinating Facts, Projects, and Activities.* Scholastic Canada LTD, 1991. Activities described in this book are easy to do and are often unique. These are provided for all areas of science, including geology.

Cole, Joanna. *The Magic School Bus® Inside the Earth.* Scholastic Inc., 1987. Ms. Frizzle takes her students on another zany adventure, this time into the center of the earth.

Davidson, Keay and A. R. Williams. *"Under Our Skin: Hot Theories on the Center of the Earth."* National Geographic, January 1996, Vol. 189, No. I. Outstanding drawings depict the most recent information regarding current theories of the interior of the earth, including motion within the mantle.

Fejer, Eva and Cecilia Fitzsimons. *An Instant Guide to Rocks Qnd Minerals.* Longmeadow Press, 1988. This easy-to-use guide to identifying minerals includes colored pictures and detailed descriptions.

Gore, Rick. *"The Dawn of Humans: Neanderthals."* National Geographic, January 1996, Vol. 189, No. 1. This article tells of the archeological dig to recover the bones of Neanderthals found in a cave in Croatia where they lived sometime between 230,000 and 300,000 years ago.

Labert, David. *The Field Guide to Geology. Facts on File, 1988.* This book is an excellent resource for teacher background. It contains information for the layperson about geology and includes very clear diagrams and drawings.

McConnell, Anita. *The World Beneath Us.* Orbis Publishing LTD, London, 1985. The great photographs and diagrams in this book give information about caves, earthquakes, and volcanoes, as well as a wide range of other topics in geology.

Peter, Carsten. *"Into the Heart of Glaciers."* National Geographic, February 1996, Vol. 189, No. 2: 70–82. The photographs in this article take the reader into a dramatic world of caves in glaciers in Greenland and the tip of South America.

Stone, William. *"Cave Quest."* National Geographic, September 1995, Vol. 188, No. 3. This article covers the adventure of cave explorers in Mexico in a mile-deep cave, the world's deepest caverns found thus far. Photographs and diagrams bring this story to life.

Van Cleave, Janice. Earth S*ciencefor Every Kid.* John Wiley and Sons, 1991. This is a book filled with easy-to-do activities to help readers understand concepts about rocks and minerals, crustal movement, and other geological topics.

Young, Ruth. *Hands-On Minds-On Science: Geology, Intemzediate.* Teacher Created Materials, Inc., 1994. This book includes activities related to the age and structure of the earth, as well as earthquakes.

Young, Ruth. *Hands-On Minds-On Science: Rocks and Minerals, Primary.* Teacher Created Materials, Inc., 1994. Activities in this book cover the topics of the rock cycle, earth's crust, and identification of minerals.

# Related Materials

## Specimens and Equipment

**Acorn Naturalists,** 17300 East 17th Street, #J-236, Tustin, CA 92680. (800) 422-8886
This company supplies activity and reference books and materials in all science areas, including geology.

**Carolina Biological Supply Co.,** 2700 York Road, Burlington, NC 27215. (800) 334-5551
Request a catalog of the Science and Technology for Children (STC) for inquiry-based science units. The STC unit Soils is designed for the second grade level.

**Delta Education, Inc.,** P.O. Box 3000, Nashua, NH 03061-9912. (800) 260-9577
Delta supplies rock specimens, streak plates, and activity books on rocks and minerals, erosion, and eartk movements. Request a science catalog and a copy of the Elementary Science Study (ESS) catalog.

**National Geographic Society,** P.O. Box 2118, Washington, DC 20013-2118. (800) 447-0647
Request a catalog of materials related to geology, including maps and posters.

**National Science Teachers Association (NSTA),** 1840 Wilson Blvd., Arlington, VA 22201-3000.1-800-722 NSTA
Request a catalog of materials which include posters and activity books on geology.

Items related to the topic of this book include the following:

        Posters: *The Dynamic Planet and Volcanoes*

        Activity Books: *Earthquakes and Wate); Stones, and Fossil Bones*

**PBS Home Video, Paciffc Arts, Nesmith Enterprises Inc.,** 11858 LaGrange Ave., Los Angeles, CA 90025.
PBS provides the Reading Rainbow video series, including The Magic School Bus(- Inside the Earth with narrator LeVar Burton exploring a cave with a spelunker.

**Ward's Natural Science Establishments, Inc.,** 5100 West Henrietta Rd., P.O. Box 92912, Rochester, NY 14692-9012. (800) 962-2660

Ward's provides a variety of mineral specimens and geology equipmer.t.

# Answer Key

## Looking at Sand *(page 10)*
Comparing sand and soil samples: Sand is made of crushed rock, and soil also contains crushed rock. Soil has organic material (i.e, leaves) in it. Sand does not. Both sand and some soils are about the same color.

**How are soil and sand formed?** Soil is formed by rock being broken into very tiny pieces and mixed with organic material. Sand is formed by rock that is broken down. The process of breaking rocks includes wind, water, ice, and other natural forces. This is called erosion.

## How Is a Cave Created? *(page 14)*
**Results of Egg Experiment:** When the vinegar is poured over the egg shell, bubbles appear all over the shell. These are created by the release of carbon dioxide gas as the egg shell is being dissolved by the acetic acid (vinegar). The egg may even move because of the lift created by the bubbles. Eventually, a film of white appears on the surface of the vinegar; this is from the chemical reaction of the dissolvlng. If the egg is Ieft overnight in vinegar, the shell will completely dissolve; only the outer membrane of the egg will remain to hoId the contents.

## EarthModel *(page 25)*

### LAYERS OF THE EARTH

| Layer | Estimated Percentage of the Total Earth | Thickness | Actual Percentage of the Total Earth |
|---|---|---|---|
| Crust | 5% | 38 miles (61km) (average) | 1% (rounded off) |
| Upper Mantle | *answers will vary* | 400 miles (640 km) | 10% |
| Lower Mantle | *answers will vary* | 1,400 miles (2,240 km) | 35% |
| Outer Core | *answers will vary* | 1,400 miles (2,240 km) | 35% |
| Inner Core | *answers will vary* | 750 miles (1,200 km) radius | 19% |

1. The estimate for the crust was 5% of the entire earth. The actual percentage is only about 1%, 10 times smaller than the original estimate.
2. Answers will vary.
3. The earth's crust is extremely thin when compared with the other layers.

## Why Does the Crust Move? *(page 28)*
### Water Temperature Experiment

The cold water will sink as it is dropped into the room temperature water; the hot water collects at the top of the room temperature water.

This compares to the heated magma near the earth's core rising to the top, while the magma at the top cools as it comes in contact with the crust and sinks. The reason for this is that the molecules of the materials cluster together more tightly as they cool; thus, the material becomes denser. When the material is heated, molecules move further apart, creating less dense, lighter material.

# Answer Key *(cont.)*

## Volcano Simulation *(page 34)*

As the vinegar is poured into the bottle and mixes with the baking soda, a reaction takes place which forms gas bubbles, creating pressure and forcing the liquid from the bottle. It pours over the sides of the bottle. This is caused by a chemical reaction between an acid (vinegar) and a base (baking soda). It can be reactivated by adding more vinegar.

### Example Diagram:

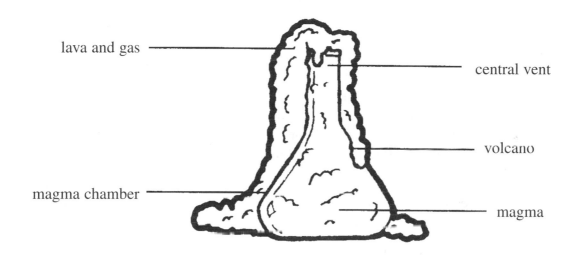

lava and gas

central vent

volcano

magma chamber

magma

## Famous Volcanoes

| Name | Location | Height | Interesting Facts |
|---|---|---|---|
| **Mount St. Helens** | Washington, U.S.A. | 8,364 feet (2,549 m) | eruped in 1980 with a blast of molten rock and hot ash which flattened forest, melted snow, and caused floods |
| **Krakatoa** | *Indonesia* | *2,667 feet (813 m)* | *great eruption in 1883 heard about 3,000 miles (4,800 km) away; produced sea waves 130 feet (40 m) high* |
| **Kilauea** | *Hawaii* | *4,000 feet (1,221 m)* | *active since 1993; lava has covered homes and added to the shoreline* |
| **Vesuvius** | *Italy* | *4,190 feet (1,277 m)* | *great eruption covered the towns of Herculaneum, Pompeii, and Stabiae in A. D. 79* |
| **Paricutin** | *Mexico* | *9,213 feet (2,808 m)* | *began in a farmer's field in 1943; built a cinder cone over 500 feet (150 m) high in six days* |
| **Stromoli** | *Mediterranean* | *3,031 feet (924 m)* | *active since ancient times; erupts constantly for months or even years at a time* |

# Glossary

**Continental Plate:** A block of the earth's crust under a continent-made mostly of granite, the plate may be up to 75 miles (120 km) thick under mountains.

**Convection Cell:** A portion of the earth's mantle heated from below and behaving like liquid boiling in a pan, it rises very slowly, spreads, cools, and sinks to be reheated and rise again. There are many cells within the mantle.

**Crust:** This outer shell of the earth rests on top of the mantle. It varies in thickness from 2 to 75 miles (3 to 120 km) with the thinnest part under the ocean and the thickest under the mountains on the continents.

**Erosion:** This is a process where ice, water, and/or wind break down a rock surface and cany away the fragments. These pieces pile up elsewhere, such as in the bottom of an ocean, and can be pressed together to form sedimentary rock.

**Igneous Rock:** It is made trom mclted rock which is torced up through a volcano or pushed into cracks in the crust where it cools into rock.

**Inner core:** An inner solid sphere within the earth surrounded by a liquid sphere, the core is made of the densest material, of iron and nickel, which settled into the center of the earth as it formed about 4.5 billion years ago. It is approximately 750 miles (1,200 km) in radius and reaches temperatures of $88,000°$ F to $13,0000°$ F ($4,400°$ C to $7,0000°$ C).

**Lava:** It is magma that has been pushed above the earth's crust. When lava comes to the surface, it is red hot and may be $2,102°$ F ($1,100°$ C) or hotter.

**Magma:** This is semimelted rock found in the mantle below the crust.

**Mantle:** It's a layer of semimolten rock with temperatures varying from $1,600°$ F to $8,0000$ F ($870°$ C to $4,4000°$ C) and reaching a depth of 1,800 miles (2,880 km) beneath the crust.

**Metamorphic Rock:** Thi.s rock was once igneous or sedimentary rock that was subjected to extreme heat and pressure and changed to a harder and more complete crystalline form.

**Outer Core:** A layer of liquid iron and nickel lying beneath the mantle, it is about 1,400 miles (2,240 km) thick and has a temperaturc range of $8,000°$ F to $11,000°$ F ($4,4000°$ C to $6,1000°$ C).

**Pangea:** This is the namc givcn to the land mass formed when the northern and southern continents were all together about 350 million years ago. They have gradually split apart to be where they are today but continue to drift.

**Plate Tectonics:** This is the theory that the earth's crust is broken into more than a dozen sections (plates) which are being shitted due to the motion of convection currents in the magma beneath the crust. Continents are areas on thc plates which rise above sea level.

**Rock Cycle:** This is a continuous cycle of rocks changing from their original forms of igneous, sedimentary, and metamorphic to any of these three types of rocks.

**Sedimentary Rock:** This is rock which has been formed by small pieces of eroded rocks which are carried by rivers and streams into lakes and oceans where it forms layers. It covers about three-fourths of the land.